Meditation

LEVEL 9

DEC●DABLES
BY jump!

Teaching Tips

Gold Level 9

This book focuses on developing reading independence, fluency, and comprehension.

Before Reading

- Ask readers what they think the book will be about based on the title. Have them support their answer.

Read the Book

- Encourage readers to read silently on their own.
- As readers encounter unfamiliar words, ask them to look for context clues to see if they can figure out what the words mean. Encourage them to locate boldfaced words in the glossary and ask questions to clarify the meaning of new vocabulary.
- Allow readers time to absorb the text and think about each chapter.
- Ask readers to write down any questions they have about the book's content.

After Reading

- Ask readers to summarize the book.
- Encourage them to point out anything they did not understand and ask questions.
- Ask readers to review the questions on page 23. Have them go back through the book to find answers. Have them write their answers on a separate sheet of paper.

© 2024 Booklife Publishing
This edition is published by arrangement with Booklife Publishing.

North American adaptations © 2024 Jump!
5357 Penn Avenue South
Minneapolis, MN 55419
www.jumplibrary.com

Decodables by Jump! are published by Jump! Library.
All rights reserved. No part of this book may be reproduced in any form without written permission from the publisher.

Library of Congress Cataloging-in-Publication Data is available at www.loc.gov or upon request from the publisher.

ISBN: 979-8-88524-793-1 (hardcover)
ISBN: 979-8-88524-794-8 (paperback)
ISBN: 979-8-88524-795-5 (ebook)

Photo Credits

Images are courtesy of Shutterstock.com. With thanks to Getty Images, Thinkstock Photo and iStockphoto. Cover – Sunil Iodhwal. p4–5 –iofoto, MintImages. p6–7 -Evgeny Atamanenko, SmartPhotoLab. p8–9 – Dmitry Kalinovsky, Africa Studio. p10–11 – kornnphoto, Quintanilla. p12–13 – wavebreakmedia, Suzanne Tucker. p14–15 –Creativa Images, Anatoliy Karlyuk. p16–17 – AnnGaysorn, Anukul. p18–19 - wavebreakmedia, jannoon028. p20–21 - Khosro, Anton Watman.

Table of Contents

Healthy You

Keeping your body healthy can mean lots of different things. It can mean eating healthy food, exercising, and resting well. One of the most important parts of staying healthy is taking care of your mind.

Your mind is the part of you that thinks, feels emotions, and remembers things. Having a healthy mind can help us in lots of ways. It may help us think clearly, make better decisions, and live better lives.

What Is Meditation?

Meditation is something useful that can help you understand your thoughts and feelings. It can be difficult to learn, but it can be very helpful when you get the hang of it!

People meditate for lots of different reasons. Some people may do it to **relax** and get rid of **stress**. Other people may do it to focus on the thoughts they have.

Yoga meditation is good exercise for your mind and your body.

Where Did Meditation Come From?

We still don't really know where meditation came from. We also cannot even be sure who used it first or how old it is. Some people believe it started thousands of years ago in India.

Today, millions of people from all around the world meditate. People might meditate in a big class or at home on their own.

Joining a class is a good way to find out if meditation is right for you.

Why Should I Meditate?

Meditation can help you in lots of ways. It can help you focus and clear your mind when you have lots to think about.

You can meditate whenever and wherever you feel comfortable.

Some people think that meditating often can help you sleep better. Some people also believe that meditation may even help your body be more fit and strong.

Getting good sleep helps you feel healthy and full of energy.

Types of Meditation

There are many different types of meditation. Different types of meditation can do different things for both your mind and your body.

Some types of meditation involve sitting down with your eyes closed.

Some types of meditation are about giving all your attention to one thing. Other types of meditation are about clearing your mind and not focusing on anything at all!

With **walking meditation**, you will focus on each step you take.

Mindfulness Meditation

Mindfulness meditation is about noticing what is happening around you and what you are thinking. Don't focus on any one thing. If a thought comes into your head, just notice it and let it move on.

In mindfulness meditation, we would only notice that we were waiting in a line rather than get annoyed at having to wait.

Try it yourself! Relax your body and try to notice things around you with each one of your senses.

Focused Meditation

Focused meditation is a little different from mindfulness meditation. In focused meditation, we try to focus our full attention on one thing. Focusing on something for a long time can be more difficult than you may think!

Let's try it out! Get yourself a drink. Now, focus on it. Is it warm or cold? Can you smell it? What does it feel like when you drink it? Every time your mind thinks about something else, return to your drink.

Guided Meditation

Guided meditation is led by someone who is not meditating. They might read from a script. They guide the person who is meditating through what to imagine and think about.

Let's try it. Ask a friend to close their eyes. Then, read this script to them:

Breathe deeply. Imagine you are on a beach. Feel the warm water on your toes. Dig them into the cool sand. The Sun's heat feels like a warm blanket on your skin. It helps your body relax.

Yoga Meditation

Yoga is an exercise for the body and the mind. When you practice yoga, you will make different shapes with your body while you focus on your breathing. The shapes are called poses, and they all have special names.

Let's try Lotus pose! Follow these instructions.

Sit with your legs in front of you.

Cross your legs.

Bring your hands to your knees and hold them like this.

Close your eyes. Breathe deeply. Focus on every breath in and out.

Index

How to Use an Index

An index helps us find information in a book. Each word has a set of page numbers. These page numbers are where you can find information about that word.

Page numbers

Example: balloons 5, <u>8–10</u>, 19

Important word

This means page 8, page 10, and all the pages in between.
Here, it means pages 8, 9, and 10.

Questions

1. Do we know where or when meditation started?

2. What is a yoga pose?

3. Can you name a good thing that meditation can do for you?

4. Can you use the Table of Contents to find information about mindfulness?

5. Using the Index, can you find which page has information about India?

6. Using the Glossary, can you define what guided meditation is?

Glossary

focused meditation:
Meditation that helps us focus our thoughts and attention.

guided meditation:
Meditation that is led by a teacher.

meditation:
The act of thinking deeply and quietly.

mindfulness meditation:
Meditation that helps us be aware and present in the moment.

relax:
To become less tense or anxious.

stress:
Mental or emotional strain or pressure.

walking meditation:
Meditation that focuses on your body's movement.

yoga:
Exercises and meditation that help us control our minds and bodies.